Praise for *Musings, Woolgathering, & Ghosts*

"CK Sobey has gifted the world with these poems and photographs that tap into our common vulnerabilities and strengths. The messages that resound throughout the book are of loving ourselves exactly as we are, connecting with others in spite of our loneliness, and minding our creative callings. I highly recommend this beautiful book of soothing words and images and am looking forward to another volume soon."

—Anne Marie Bennett, Author *Dragonflies at Night*

"From the first invitation to 'Take my hand. Let's begin,' to the poem about a reluctant dancer, Kas Sobey takes us along on the highs and lows of her own journey. She asks us to not only walk with her, but to reevaluate our own choices made over many years, to look with new eyes on what the future may hold, and to always be open to what life has to offer. The isolation of the pandemic added further opportunities to reflect, reconsider, let go, and open to new challenges and new possibilities. May you respond to her invitation with curiosity and an open heart, the way Kas lives her life. You'll be glad you did."

—Helen Rousseau, author of *Coming to the Edge*
and *Poems for a World on Fire*

"The book you hold in your hands is walking permission and divine inspiration for every person with a story to share: Write it! Photograph it! Publish it! Kas's muse carries you across the threshold of your fears into the realm of poetry, photography, and prose as it reconnects you to Nature and your one authentic and wild life. In these pages, Kas lives and captures the story she was born to tell as she 'unravels the old and sets sail on the wind of future possibilities.' May we all."

—Edveeje Fairchild, M.Ed., Founder of A Woman's Nature School
Founding Chief Operations Officer of TreeSisters

"A very thoughtful book that would be a good read anytime, but one that works especially well during these turbulent, trying times. For sure I will be returning to many passages for second and third looks, reflecting once again."

—Howard Rice

More Praise for *Musings, Woolgathering, & Ghosts*

"This is a profoundly beautiful book, written by a profoundly beautiful soul. It will touch you, open you, hold you, uplift you, delight you, and illuminate you. Kas's unbridled love for all of Life can be viscerally felt in these exquisite offerings of image and word. Some of it will take your breath away, some of it will make you smile in kindred knowing, some of it will open you to questions your soul is eager for you to explore. All of it will nourish you. This is a book to treasure."

—Suzanne Eder,
Alchemy of Self-Love Teacher, Author, and Guide

"Do not let the deceptively simple language of these prose poems fool you. The questions Kas asks are those of the deepest mysteries of the human heart, unable to be answered and yet ripe for the musing, which Kas does exquisitely in this collection. Each poem is a meditation to be savored slowly and soulfully."

—Susannah Crolius, Founder, art + soul

"In *Musings, Woolgathering, and Ghosts,* CK Sobey conveys her deep connection and commitment to nature, spirituality, and solitude. Through her innermost contemplations, her wisdom guides, her questions inspire, and her vulnerability is heartfelt. The ebb and flow of her calm welcoming voice and the mystical allure in her photographs invite the reader to her human and spiritual journey and nature's rhythms of life."

—Anna Bozena Bowen, Author of *HATTIE,* a novel

"This beautiful collection inspires awe, appreciation, and admiration. Delightful insights on life in its many forms, and the beauty and mystery of the world that surrounds us are accompanied by sensitively composed photographs. I'm sure that I will want to return to find inspiration here time and again."

—Clive Johnson, Spiritual teacher and writer

Musings,
Woolgathering,
& Ghosts

Poetic prose and photographs by
CK Sobey

INNER HARVESTING

Musings, Woolgathering, & Ghosts: Poetic and Visual Offerings from My Life to Yours
2021 © CK Sobey
ISBN 978-1-7375061-0-2

Cover and all interior photographs by CK Sobey

Cover and book design by Lindy Gifford

Editing by Genie Dailey

Inner Harvesting, Publisher
www.innerharvesting.com

November 2022
Dear Shelley,
"May you find inspiration, joy + spiritual reflection as you enjoy these books!"
Kas

This book is dedicated to every person who still holds their dreams close and dear.

Continue to cherish them, for they will be your North Star.

For those of you who continue forward with your visions and dreams.

Who are not too timid to adjust to the winds of change.

Keep a hunger to express life in your own way.

Here's to Life!

Much love,
CK (Kas) Sohey

Foreword

There is nothing more powerful than an idea whose time has come.

—Howard Thurman

I had been in a cocoon of solitude for over two years.
When the Coronavirus arrived, the forced isolation already felt familiar.
To give room for what was happening, I started slowing down
my professional life.
I emptied the busy parts of my life slowly at first, then completely.
I allowed this essential need to empty me.
To take me along in its quest.
What had once given me passion and meaning to meet the day had changed.
This affected me on a deeper, personal level as well.

Something wanted to emerge. I gave it the space and waited.

I took more walks, did my best to invite the solitude in as a co-creator.
I began to realize that in this space of personal, and soon-to-be-forced,
isolation, I wrote more than I ever had. My writing had changed as well.
I asked some trusted friends to read some of what I had written.

Then the book began.

Actually, this book began years ago. I just didn't know it then.

I believe the creative spirit yearns for ideas to be born. Regardless
of how the creative spirit shows up—writing, cooking, gardening—

if it is ignored, it will find someone else to give it life. This notion has been written about by others. I know this to be true for me, too. I have done my best to tap into my creative muses and show them the respect and delight they flourish in.

I have moved to different homes with my ever-expanding folders filled with notes, stories, and ideas written in notebooks, on scraps of paper, and on whatever I could find when my muse visited me with gifts of inspiration.

More recently, I have gone back to those files with a sharper eye and found many that had worthwhile stories to tell. I continued where the words took me.

Not always in stories, but shorter pieces of a poetic prose: musings. My fingers tapping away at the keyboard with their own will or composing with a pen.

The words usually weaving themselves into uncharted places I had not necessarily planned.

I enjoyed rediscovering my creative muses. I wrote, doodled, which I found helps my creative process unfold.

I walked a lot, and took photographs of what I saw that affected, stimulated, and aroused me. I needed aliveness around me when COVID arrived. That was hard to find. I walked and waved at people. They waved back. That was life during the first year of the pandemic. But I felt an even stronger sense of union with nature on my walks. Perhaps because it was all I had that was alive, as my pets had gone. Those walks filled me up. I hope I have conveyed that feeling of inspiration to my writing.

This book contains many of those musings.

My wanderings in my thoughts and heart space are different.
Some are deeper, more insightful. Others are lighter and more playful.
Some are haunting, with vivid memories that follow me through my life.
I hope that everyone who is drawn to this book will resonate in some
way with the stories on these pages.

Throughout the book, I have blended some of my photography that I
feel forms a relationship with my musings. The pictures alone also tell
their own stories.

What I find again and again is that even the most ordinary of my days
hold magic and gifts. The *un*-ordinary is always waiting to be noticed.

Read this book from cover to cover, a bit at a time, or stroll around in
the sections. I hope my book touches you in ways that generate good
and nourishing feelings in many ways.

CK Sobey
Valley Forge, Pennsylvania
Spring 2021

Contents

Perhaps everything that frightens us is in its deepest essence something helpless that wants our love.

—Rainer Maria Rilke

Beginning Again

I am at a threshold again.

Which way to go?

Which path to take?

The more challenging one, of course.

Beginning again.

Stories woven with richness and texture.

Incredible odysseys.

Will you journey with me this time into the next chapter of life?

Let's begin to unravel the old.

Sail on the winds of future possibilities together.

What will we decide to keep?

What will be swept away?

I will ask for lightheartedness.

Where to begin?

Anywhere we want.

We may feel lost at times.

We're not.

Take my hand.

Let's begin.

MUSINGS

A Conversation of Deeper Proportions

I have read that trees communicate with each other.
Years ago, I studied the practice of Silva Mind Control
and I was also immersing myself in Shamanic studies.
At different points in both studies, I was told to place my hands
on the body (trunk) of a tree.
I was instructed to quiet myself, totally,
outside and within.
I was told to listen.
To wait and sense what came through.

I remember standing in front of a big, beautiful old grandfather tree.
I did as I was told. With eyes closed, I listened to what the tree told me.
I started to enter a place of shared intelligence with the tree.
I felt at peace.
In a place of agreement.
After a while, how long I cannot say, I realized
multiple thoughts and reflections were flowing into me.
It was awesome, unbelievable.
That was long ago.

This story begins on a walk weeks ago.
It had been a long time since I had listened to the trees in an intimate way.
Living in a world of the ongoing isolation of COVID precautions,
I haven't been able to see anyone close up,
to touch or hold a hand, to hug another human being.
My life of talking and listening currently, as for many of us,
is to share stories and thoughts in a Zoom room.
I enjoy isolation more than most, but I get incredibly lonely some days.

I made this walk's intention to initiate an intimate conversation with a tree.

As I walked with curiosity, I watched for some tree to signal me.

I was stunned by the lack of life energy all around.

Then I found a large tree beckoning me, again and yet again, as I walked by it.

"Come to me," the tree said. Or this is how I interpreted it.

I walked over, spoke a blessing,

then placed my palms on its trunk.

I began to breathe more deeply.

To relax.

I waited for what was to come.

Words do not quite do the trick in this type of union.

Let me share with you the best I can as I write this.

The Tree was shimmering with joy to talk with me.

The Tree was explaining that I shouldn't worry so much

about appearances with regard to the trees everywhere.

That there is a remarkable underground network

of communication where chemicals and signals are sent

to other trees through their root systems.

Different species of trees are interconnected

through one spectacular root system.

This dynamic system spans all over the world.

The Tree went on to explain that there is

much death and damage being done above the ground.

That because of the root system all over the world,

there will never be annihilation to the trees.

I can't tell you how long the tree spoke to me.

Many trees seem asleep energetically.

This is because of the approaching winter, when they go deeply within.

Many trees appear to be dying and they are, but only in appearance.

Their life energy is going into this vast, vibrant root system
to continue into the future.
That this whole underground network will rise,
once again, to blanket the earth with unimaginable species.
I was amazed at the brilliance of what has been going on for ages.
When our time was ending, I thanked the Tree and walked on.

My walk was more grounded. My steps lighter.
I looked around me with an inner sight.
A different, softer lens.
As Abraham Maslow said, and I paraphrase here,
"the sacred is in the ordinary..."
When I walk now, I know that appearances are just that.
Below the surface of what I see is a world within itself.
Strong and alive.
Now I look deeper and listen.
I walk on sacred ground.

A Walk Most High

"What is it that troubles and concerns you, my child?" he asked me.

All I could see around me was green grass, clouds, and exquisite birds.

It was very peaceful where I was.

Why now?

Why, when I had called out to anyone, why show up now?

I answered him, "Please help me release some of the pain and pressure.

I feel I am lost in my life's journey. I want to breathe freely again."

There was a radiant, shimmering aura around him.

He asked, "Do you know me?"

I answered, "Yes, you are the Christ."

"I am one of many messengers and many forms

sent to this earth to guide and help when needed."

We walked for a time; I could not even tell you for how long.

I felt such peace and calm.

I felt unruffled.

"Thank you for coming," I said.

"I am always here, dear one, a breath away.

Split wood, I am there. Lift up a rock, you will find me there."

And all was well.

I breathe differently now.

I have calmed and quieted my soul. —Psalms 131:2

And It Came to Pass

And it came to pass throughout the land,
an idea was born.
The idea grew among people and creatures alike.
Many were against the idea and could not wrap their minds around it.
Their hearts had become tiny and dry.
Some grew beyond this narrow way of life.
They joined the growing number of people encouraged by the idea.
Some became silent and preferred to use other means
to receive and share the idea.
Unrest grew throughout the land.
This unrest grew in numbers.
In the end, or the beginning, the idea begun so long ago prevailed.
The losses were significant in many ways.
The gains were more.
The idea was peace.

Corona Walking

Sitting in my quiet, again,
another day to take part in.
I will not permit the isolation to break me,
I will not disappear into the aloneness.
I will respect it and acknowledge its power,
make it my friend.

How long till I can hug someone?
Till I can touch someone?
Will I hear laughter in my home?
How long till that time?
Till a glass of wine with a friend?

The answers are unknown,
for this is a time for inventiveness,
patience, and prayer.
What knowledge will be gained when life begins again,
when this ends.
I will seek others out with more kindness;
I will see them.
I promise.

I will not take my walks for granted.
The birds serenade me,
praying that I may hear them tomorrow.
I walk seeing so much more.

In Search of the Grail

What if the grail really existed?

That it held the answers to our questions about God, Spirit, the Universe?

All the answers for all the questions asked through the ages?

Answers uncomplicated in their fundamental nature.

So significant in its simplicity.

Why had Percival searched for this treasure for so many years of his life?

His noble promise to his king and all he held sacred.

It is my belief that we all search for this treasured

vessel of truth at different junctures in our lives.

That we can be guided in mysterious ways that offer us a chance to awaken.

That the treasure may be a breath away.

Instead, we learn to obey.

To listen to what we are told.

If we learn well, our lives become routine in mind and deed.

Different rewards to bind us to do even better.

Every day marching to the same drummer.

Our craving to search for the value of life is a distant memory.

But now and then, something shines through.

Cracks begin to open and let some light in.

We become curious and look deeper.

Is there a place within us that holds the treasure we all seek?

I believe this.

It is a place where our grail waits to be found.

I Rise, Again

Shall I tell you of my secret place?
I will share this with you because I trust you
to hold my secret close to your heart.
It becomes your secret now as well;
please protect it.

I go to this place when there is pain in my heart,
when my vulnerability has been compromised, for she is tender.
I go when I am beaten down.

I enter this place of essential stillness.
It envelops me,
disillusionment, angst surround me no more.
I rise!

My antenna warns me of approaching danger,
someone's need to conquer,
being overtaken by outer circumstances.
Any inner demons that may revisit find no opening.
I rise!

I stand and listen to the gentle wind,
whispering eternal secrets to my deepest core.
I rise, again!

Needing to Believe

We all need something to believe in.
There seems to be a startling rate of humanity
needing to understand what's going on.

No man is an island—
we need each other,
we belong to each other, this planet.
We all cast our hopes in quiet requests,
morning prayers, and outrageous demands.

Something good, authentic, and powerful is beginning,
slowly and mightily, it is traveling from the west to the east, north and south.
Sometime soon, there will be more extraordinary moments on this planet,
too numerous to stand alone and disregard.

These moments will blossom into beautiful stretches of grace
and unity felt throughout.
Growing numbers will begin to participate.
But not today. Not yet.

Offerings

The waiter stood tall and proud as he spoke
about the daily specials for dinner.
I felt I was in an audience watching an intimate one-man show.
He glanced down at his notes to review.
Then he continued with his performance.
Each selection was deliciously described.
He looked right in my eyes as he spoke.

By the end, I was spellbound.
How to choose one dish over the other?
Would my palate be satisfied with just one choice?
The blue cheeseburger was not a daily special.
I could not meet the waiter's eyes when I ordered.
He smiled into mine and said, "Good choice," and winked.

I have come to realize that every day offers me something special.
Usually, more than one option,
but at least one unique choice.
My choices are seldom easy or pleasant,
but eventually are agreeable to me.

If they're not, my stomach reacts unfavorably to the decision.
It may take hours for it to speak up, but eventually, it does.

The blue cheeseburger seems easier to digest.
Choosing the right selection to eat is a lot like life.

Prayer to the Four Directions

Mother, Father, Great Spirit, God of my Understanding,
I ask for your blessing and strength as I place myself in your loving hands.

I face the East.
The direction and place of newness and spontaneity.
I ask to join in partnership with all the powers
of playful discovery and curiosity.
To find my place within, to express my life's creativity in countless ways.

I face the South.
Land of loving warmth and calming breezes that ease me.
Where I find peace in the green leaves of Mother Tree, and
sacred walks along the sands of contemplation.
You are my solace, my great retreat when I need it the most.
It is here I align my intentions and life purpose.

I face the West, where I review my life with vigor and respect.
I sense the changing of my life's seasons here.
Realizing and knowing that I am wiser and hopefully kinder.
At this time, I re-collect memories gathered throughout this great journey.
I choose to celebrate what I have uncovered in this time of my life.
Finding joy when my opposing parts begin to dance together,
birthing new ways of inventiveness.
I celebrate my life!

I face the North, as I know the winds of great change await me.
I ask for the courage and faith to know I am soon crossing
the Great Divide between Earth and what is still unknown to me.
I will discover love so profound, huge, and comforting, I will find no words.
Speechless, I will rest and gather in this divine universe of abundance.
My guardians and guides will be by my side as they have been my whole life.
I delight in the next experience when the time comes.

Thank you.

The Retrieval of a Soul

Where does my Soul go when I spend too much time in the dark?
When the hurts of my heart begin to smolder and burn?
Does my Soul shrink and shrivel?
Does it disappear to some place never wanting to be found?
Does it fracture?
Can it get lost, forever?
I don't believe so.
My Soul has packed up and left me at times.
But only for lengthy stays.
Not permanently.
Until I went to retrieve it,
to call it home to wholeness.
Large amounts of coaxing and apologies will get the communication going.
Sincerity and honesty are necessary for my Soul to believe in me,
to feel safe with the choices I make, again.

This dance of ours will take place many times in my life.
Being human is not for sissies.
Does my Soul grow and expand with life, with my experiences?
I believe it travels with me through time.
If I don't go searching, it will stay away.
Hiding in shattered areas, waiting to be retrieved,
to be made whole.
I promise to always retrieve it from the shadows.

Walking with Pavarotti

Yesterday, the clouds traveled across the sky,
blocking the sun from warming my face.
Growing in intensity, angry.
Every day my emotions change quickly. Like the clouds.

Meandering in the park, listening to Pavarotti through earbuds.
Pavarotti growing in passionate song.
I felt my anticipation also growing at the approaching rain.
My feet continued walking themselves.
The earth beneath my feet felt particularly sacred yesterday.
Walking with Pavarotti.
The clouds started to open.
Not to the expected rain, but to sun.
Raising my face, I smiled.
The rain didn't arrive.
Joy arrived instead.
Highs and lows like the changing weather.
Solitude being my new partner during this time of contagion.
I continued my walk,
Pavarotti playing on.
The sun shining down.
All seemed right with my smaller world.

WOOLGATHERING

.

A Good Day

There is a different quality about today;
my sensory levels feel alive.
It is not a place of frustration and distant hopelessness;
the everyday isolation that brings loneliness with it
is not hovering today.
Nope, not today.
Today I see with softer eyes;
walking, I watch the leaves float gracefully to the ground.
Autumn fullness.
The magic of slower motion in play.

This ground where others walk with collections of private thoughts,
the cooler breezes carrying messages of love, hope.
A generosity of Spirit.
The geese are in full flight toward winter homes in the south.
Do they faithfully carry messages to other geese?
Are others gazing at these geese also?
This thought fills me with joy,
this mystical experience that has been going on through generations.

Wherever one is on the planet sky-gazing, somewhere, someone else is, too.
I love thinking this.
Feelings of unity and security come to mind
while I spend time with this notion.
This is a great day.

A Small Ritual

I catch a dream in my hand.
The time is just before evening dusk.
The warm glow opening up a world of promise.
I bring my hand closer.
I notice my skin is getting thinner.
Finer, softer like silk.
It has a luminescence.
The dream is ready to be born.
I open my hand and make a wish,
allowing it to fly free.

Alchemy

I'm glad it didn't go as I had planned.

A little easier would have been nice.

But then I wouldn't have found that my heart could go so deep.

Stretch so wide.

That I was strong and resilient.

And through the pain, find another love.

Me.

What would have happened if everything had worked out that way I planned?

I don't know.

It didn't.

An Idea

I am an idea.
I inspire and ignite people to create.
My next project involves building a relationship with a particular pen.
This will succeed because the pen wishes me
to flow freely from its proud fountain of ink.
We will work together to create pages upon pages of a story.

At times, my new friend can be very argumentative.
Not wanting to flow easily with what I share.
I'm hoping the pen is able to move past any blocks that may arise.
I become frustrated when I impart my ideas and they are ignored.
If it takes too long to notice me, I will leave to find
someone else who will be stirred by me.

I come in many forms.
I delight when I see a soul excited with what I bring.
I have inspired great gardens and timeless architecture.
Imaginative books, poems, and quotes.
Recipes for meals that became famous
and many that remain in families for generations.
I have initiated walks along simple trails that changed lives.
I always have been and will be forever.

When I visit you, please take a moment to notice me.
Sometimes I am so huge, you may find it hard to breathe.
Spend some time with me.
Let's figure out what you want to do with me.

Flight Plan Humor

Connection requested with self:
Step one,
close eyes.
Step two,
walk faster.
Step three,
open arms wide.
Liftoff!
Success.
Flying.
Step four,
come in for a landing,
check alignment.
Step five,
open eyes, peek.
Step six,
sight target,
preferred destination straight ahead,
bench nestled among trees.
Step seven,
land.
Step eight,
sit on bench.
Step nine,
go within.
Inner connection established,
soft eyes confirmed.
"I need to talk."
"I know, I am here."

Reminiscing

Small joys today.
Someone smiled at me with their eyes,
their whole face lighting up.
I smiled in response.

Crossing the pedestrian walk, every car slowed down and stopped.
I waved thanks;
they all waved back, mostly.

Kmart is closing in my area;
the neighborhood is talking about this.
Reminiscing.

I went to visit the store today and mourn.
I walked along the aisles, looking at the soon-to-be-orphaned carts.
I listened to people just talking to themselves,
the aisles echoing with the hum of voices.
In the checkout line, we spoke with each other—
community grief.
Everyone walked away with prizes;
my neighborhood was at their best that day.
I will remember this for a long time.

The Way of a Snail

Snails sleep up to three years. Do snails dream?

What do they dream of?

Does a snail wake up wondering about the changes in its landscape?

The snail carries its home on its back.

How brilliant is that?

I don't fall asleep easily, or sleep for long lengths of time.

Staying deeply asleep for a long time would be a sweet lullaby for me.

I can imagine feeling the transformation that would occur

as I slipped into sleep.

Lovely.

A soft slide into a place of trust.

Not an everyday occurrence in my world.

If ever.

Too much going on too often.

When I nap in the in-between hours, it is like that.

Drifting into warm sunlight.

A voyage to the stars. Dancing with moonbeams.

Spellbinding.

"To sleep—perchance to dream," was not placed in my human toolbox.

Or, I have yet to find my own unique instructions.

Are the solutions to this mystery right in front of me?

Can I carry my home with me?

Learn to sleep wherever I meander to?

Perhaps I should lighten my load.

Be more like the snail.

Tucker Wisdom

For those of us who have pets to watch, it's a fascinating pastime.
I watched our cat Tucker this morning. Longer than usual.
He was in a regal pose.
Was he dreaming of a long-ago memory when he was
the guardian of some ancient wilderness?
Does he revisit that ancient land?
Was he revered?
He certainly looks the part.
I wonder, when I speak to Tucker of Sophie, does he recall her?
Does it bring back memories of their shared turbulent, territorial times?
I believe animals have souls.
I am sure of this.
Their personalities are uniquely different.
Will they live again?
The veil that divides the here and the hereafter
may include the animal kingdom as well.
Not only entrusted to the human race.
My vote is yes.
I notice Tucker is looking at me as if to say,
"Oh, don't bother yourself with such thoughts.
I am cozy on your lap.
Relax in the luxurious sun with me."
Tucker wisdom.

A Bedtime Story

Little one, bedtime is calling, and the moon is rising.
Let us gaze at her together and see how she adorns
the night sky with precious jewels.
Mother Moon is wrapping her loving light
and magic around you and all who notice.
If you close your eyes and listen in the silence,
you will hear her speaking to you.
Whispering of shimmering stardust,
wondrous dreams and ideas filled with magic.
A dream awaits you, darling child.
Let yourself go, and trust her loving mantle of moonbeams.
She will keep you safe through this night,
till you decide to awaken to the new day.

GHOSTS

Ghosts

Memories are like ghosts.

Events tucked in between today and yesterday.

On occasion, they visit us,

reminding us of something rare we've experienced.

Years ago, on a walk up a steep hill,

I spied a pair of tiny slippers

thoughtfully placed side by side.

Who did they belong to?

Why would someone leave them on the hill?

I have heard it said that when we least expect it, something happens.

Unexpected, unusual events occur.

On a particularly hot day, I saw a big turtle ahead of me

on the asphalt path, not moving.

Not knowing if it was dead or alive, I increased my pace and picked it up.

I picked it up and searched for signs of life.

Nothing. I hoped it was asleep due to the heat.

Then, as in response, it slowly drew its neck back into its shell.

I carried this precious bundle over to a pond that appears after heavy rains.

I rubbed my finger along the underside,

wondering if the turtle would sense I meant no harm.

I put the turtle down, in a shaded wet area by the pond,

sure this was where it originally was on its way to.

To this day I look for some sign of the turtle,

wondering what happened.

One afternoon, driving along a back road, I saw something ahead of me.
I slowly maneuvered around, careful not to drive over it.
I saw it was a robin that seemed stuck to the blacktop.
I made a hurried U-turn, praying the few cars
behind me would not run over it.
Pulling up behind the bird, I put my hazard lights on
and stepped out of my car.
Bending down, I gently picked it up, flailing, not able to fly away.
I remember reading somewhere that birds scare easily.
This can cause their heart to stop.
A wing was severely injured.
Cupping it in my hand, cooing and stroking, I placed it
under a large, leafy sheltering tree far off the road.

I heard a horn beep and looked to see a line of cars behind mine.
The car behind mine had been watching all this unfold.
Witnessing this moment.
Another person got out of their car and stood watching.
There was a sense of quiet wonderment encircling us.
I placed the robin under the tree.
To this day, when I drive by that tree,
I wonder if there was more I should have done.

Did anyone come back for the little slippers?
Are they still there?
I will never know.
I moved away the next week.
The ghosts visit me on occasion.

Ancestral Dreaming

If you will, allow your mind to wander,
become a benign witness.
Notice life around you.
Marvel at all this life we have lived through so far.
Raging tears at injustice, stupidity some view as trivia.
Unbelievable loving care that flows forth from strangers.
Belly laughs and joy.
There really aren't any strangers in the book of life.
The veil of differences between us is sheer.
Why are we so often thick-headed?
Some of us love to experience the roller coaster of life.
Or a smooth, measured existence is more often sought after.
What roots of lineage are ingrained in our DNA?
Maybe we are all the same family?
What journeys are still to come?
Even now unfolding?
Can we look forward with anticipation?
Or are we too exhausted?
There may be a gentle, skillful nudging that moves us forward.
That helps us on our meandering voyage of life.
We are not alone.
Never alone.

A Yield of Plenty

At times there is so much want inside us.
We are not satisfied with life.
With what we have.
We forget to notice the little things.
The things that are little treasures we generally would cherish.

"Not enough; more," we start to think too often.
"They have plenty more than I have. I want more.
Now."
"When will my time of plenty arrive?" we ask impatiently.
"I deserve it.
Probably more than most," we say.
"Why do I always have to give?
Why me?"

We live our life day to day,
just existing.
We forget how to harvest our yield of plenty.

Our thoughts become enraged.
Our hearts, numb.
"Why me?"
We become overwhelmed by everything.
We forget.

My grandmother had a plaque in her kitchen.
It was over the sink where she washed the dishes.
DO UNTO OTHERS.
I would sneak in the kitchen and read it over and over.
It made me feel like I had a secret.

Gathering my yield of plenty starts with a small gesture.
Could I live like that?
To simply feel I had plenty?
Maybe that's all I need.

Behind Me

Oftentimes, I revisit my past.
I view screenshots of my life,
some moments being more insightful.
I don't analyze my past decisions much anymore.
They were actions of my past.
I did the best I could with what I knew.
My past is where I began to understand discernment.
In slow, aching small steps.
What's behind me still revisits.
Acceptance of decisions made is a great ally to me.
The crazy days of the '60s and the dawning
of the consciousness movement.
Soft Florida nights, scented breezes, drugs,
close encounters, and heart awakening.
The edgy years of reaching enlightenment
till I couldn't see the light anymore.
Friends never to return and new ones entering.
Discovering the words I say to myself are actually heard on a cellular level.
What was behind me shaped my vision of life.
Life constantly changes, as do I.
The past has taught me to cast brilliance in unique ways.
What's behind me drives me forward.
Life's bumpy ride gives texture to my life.
What's behind me propels me to seek what's beckoning.

A Letter of Love

I think you should know I love you.
I think you should know how much you are cared for.
How gifted you are.
I think you should know how grand life can be.
This is true.
How much fun there is waiting for you!
Life is many things and all the in-between.
How big and wide will you live your life?
Or will the fear of this day cause your experience to be narrowed, smaller?
Starvation is not always about the stomach.
It is all about the view.

To love fully can be heartbreaking.
Yet it can be more about heart-opening.
This is real life.
Really.

Be open to the giggles and sobs.
Stretch yourself to experience life, even for a day, an hour.
Something you want more often!
Become greedy for.
Crave it every day!

Create the life you want.
Mambo or long waltzes into the morning light!
Let juices drip down your chin for the sheer joy of the experience!
Whatever may be happening, be there fully.
Make it yours!
Your time, your life.

Nothing lasts forever.
Take the next step.
It is just that. The next step.
I think you should know how grand life can be.
I think you should know how much I love you.

Beside the Sea

Beside the sea, we sat looking out at the waves moving gently in and out.

A beautiful, radiant rising sun as a zenith in this expectant moment.

Beside the sea, he softly spoke of love.

That he wanted to spend his life with me.

He spoke of the dreams he had for us.

My breaths became fuller, fueling my heart's growing intoxication.

He held my hand, looked deeply in my eyes.

"There is no other," he said.

Beside the sea, we promised to join forever in this life's journey.

Beside the sea, it seemed so simple.

It has become more precious with the ticking of time passing.

I will treasure these moments forever.

Little did I know my heart would break many times.

Breaking open and expanding that day beside the sea.

Coming of Age

I want to dance in the moonlight being held by strong, loving arms.
I want to move in rhythm with someone, a heartbeat away from mine.
I am just realizing, you will not be there.
I want to travel to ancient lands, to unimaginable places I have never seen.
Into my imagination with you, but you will not be there.
You never have been.
I want to laugh and cook and share the joys
and heartaches of my day with you.
I want to hear about your day, with no judgment, only insight and caring.
What happened to us?
My humiliation at your silence, your disregard of my feelings.

Early on, I wore the mask of seduction.
It began to wear thin.
Ragged.
I am growing out of my old skin.
Love is many things.
I am just realizing love can never be destroyed.
I want to continue to dance in the moonlight.
I know you will not be there.
At least, not with me.
I am coming to love myself more each day.
Thank you for helping me reach this place, in the only way you could.

I Should Have Said

Is it past the time to wonder about any of this?
Who cares anyway?
I could have changed it all if I had spoken up,
taken the right steps in the beginning.
Or maybe the steps I took were exactly right for me;
the mood of what was developing might have changed.
Is the fabric of my life different because I should have said something?
Anything?
I should have spoken up,
but maybe I did in the only way I could at the time.
I should have said goodbye long ago.

Night

Too many thoughts,
deep feelings moving around.
My leg muscles twitchy with trapped energy.
If I were a horse, I would gallop along the shore,
ride into the rough waves, and gaze at the moon in tribute.
If I were a wolf, I would howl,
howl at the beauty of it all.
As I lie here, I wait for the night to take me.
Kindness in my dreams would be a blessing.

Shadow and Light

In the depths of solitude awaits a kind of madness.
I resist it when it comes calling,
when I feel it looming.

It summoned me of its arrival the other day,
completely enveloping me.
Where did my grand plans of retreat go?
Somewhere in the dark shadows, I imagine.
So I dove in, removed my armor of ego and stood naked before it.

Hopelessness and a river of tears accompanied me,
sorrow burst forth in gagging sobs.

On the edges of this black hell came tiny bursts of light;
an invisible circle was drawn around me,
reminding me there was support, somewhere.

Knowing this gave me strength, fearlessness.
Serenity will come,
maybe even today.

The Dancer

She hides from life.
She thinks of herself in the second person.
This is always a successful place to not be noticed.
She is safe then.
Music is one way to express what is hiding.
When she moves her body into a dance,
it becomes a rhapsody for all who witness.
It is then she opens up, receives the gifts.
She allows herself to set free all that hides in the cave of her soul.
It is then she shares her story.
She hides nothing.
It is magnificent.

Acknowledgments

I want to thank many people who have been a part of writing this book. I could write a book by itself with all the stories of friendship, support, and honest discussion through the years that have been the backbone of this book.

You know who you are. There are too many to list here. You are awesome and I am blessed to have you in my life!

I want to thank Howard Rice, who has taught me in ten years what the human spirit and writer within is capable of. Howard, you have shown me and countless other writers what can be creatively accomplished in ten minutes of quick-fire writing.

It is one the most refreshing writing groups I have ever had the joy to be a part of. Thank you, Howard, for also creating a sense of trust and camaraderie between all of us.

I am also fortunate to enjoy exceptional mentors during my life. These gifted women have acted as midwives and advisers that brought my creative muses to the forefront so I could recognize them. Thank you, Cat, Suzanne, Jill, and Anne Marie. Once again, there are many more. Please know that I know who you are and how I have benefited from our connection.

To my husband, whose support and constructive comments always added some extra spice to our chats! Thank you for your patience and listening prowess to the countless stories I read to you. Thank you, Ron!

To Lindy Gifford of Manifest Identity, who listened and read the words that I wrote. Your suggestions and professionalism brought this book to the light of day through your experience and vision of what it could be. Thank you for being an outstanding collaborator to have by my side through it all. I look forward to blazing new trails with your honesty and guidance beside me.

And lastly, to Genie Dailey of Fine Points Editorial Services, who took my writing and gave it the gift of flow without taking the "me" out of the stories.

About CK Sobey

CK (Kas) Sobey continues to live
a life of curiosity.
She considers herself to be seeker.
An explorer.
Her many ventures in life attest to this.
In her earlier years she was in the
entertainment field.

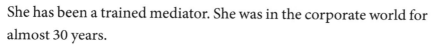

She has been a trained mediator. She was in the corporate world for
almost 30 years.
She trained as a Spiritual practitioner, and later became a certified
hypnotherapist bringing a deeper understanding of the inner mind.
She has facilitated many groups in a variety of subjects and collage art
for years.

Kas has since "retired" from her businesses to spend more time
reimagining her life.
Writing has become an important creative channel.
She enjoys cooking, walking, dancing, photography,
and exploring the planet and new ideas.
Bubble baths and a mixture of music is her way of unwinding
at the end of a day.
For the past 20 years, Kas has lived in the Valley Forge area
of Pennsylvania.
She is seeking that which is calling her to new paths.
She is presently working on a new book of tiny tales
while continuing to doodle.